ISBN 978-0-265-08372-7
PIBN 10947861

1 MONTH OF
FREE
READING

at

www.ForgottenBooks.com

By purchasing this book you are eligible for one month membership to ForgottenBooks.com, giving you unlimited access to our entire collection of over 1,000,000 titles via our web site and mobile apps.

To claim your free month visit:

www.forgottenbooks.com/free947861

English
Français
Deutsche
Italiano
Español
Português

www.forgottenbooks.com

Mythology Photography **Fiction**
Fishing Christianity **Art** Cooking
Essays Buddhism Freemasonry
Medicine **Biology** Music **Ancient**
Egypt Evolution Carpentry Physics
Dance Geology **Mathematics** Fitness
Shakespeare **Folklore** Yoga Marketing
Confidence Immortality Biographies
Poetry **Psychology** Witchcraft
Electronics Chemistry History **Law**
Accounting **Philosophy** Anthropology
Alchemy Drama Quantum Mechanics
Atheism Sexual Health **Ancient History**
Entrepreneurship Languages Sport
Paleontology Needlework Islam
Metaphysics Investment Archaeology
Parenting Statistics Criminology
Motivational

Historic, archived document

Do not assume content reflects current
scientific knowledge, policies, or practices.

U. S. DEPT. OF AGRICULTURE
OFFICE OF SUPPLY,CCC
150 BROADWAY, NEW YORK 7 NEW YORK

Cleared by:
New York, Philadelphia, Boston
Regional OWI with a "B" rating

Issued:
August 1, 1945

THE FAMILY CANTEEN

Canning with Company

ANNOUNCER:

With the prosepects of the fresh vegetable crops better
than last year's and with a bumper crop of Southern
peaches, it is up to all of us to can all we can. Some
of us lack space and equipment for home canning. But that
shouldn't stop us, for in many communities there are some
kind of canning facilities that are open for all to use.
I am, of course, referring to the Community Canning
Centers. Today, we have with us Mr. _____of the USDA's
Office of Supply. Mr. _____is going to discuss the
Community Canning Centers, what advantages they hold over
home canning, and how to start a community center, if one
is not established in your locality.

OFFICE OF SUPPLY:

First, _____, I should like to say a word about those
vegetable crops that you mentioned. This year we have a
good supply of fresh vegetables. In fact, this year's
supply is 4 per cent over last year's and 11 per cent
over the prewar years.

UNITED STATES DEPARTMENT OF AGRICULTURE
SURPLUS MARKETING ADMINISTRATION
WASHINGTON, D. C.

FOOD STAMP PLAN

SURPLUS COMMODITIES BULLETIN

Announcer: Well, it sounds as though we shouldn't let any of them

go to waste.

O. S.   No, _____, that's right. Espceially, since there will

be about 19 per cent <u>less</u> commercially canned vegetables

available for <u>civilians</u> than there were last year.

Because of the drop in commercially canned vegetables,

we should all make every effort to put up everything that

we can't use fresh from our victory gardens, and we should

take advantage of the fresh vegetables as they arrive on

the market.

Announcer:

When they're in abundant supply, they're usually less

expensive, too.

O. S.

Yes, _____that's right.

Announcer: Garden fresh vegetables are best for canning when they

are fresh picked at the peak of eating quality.

O.S.   Right again _____,

UNITED STATES DEPARTMENT OF AGRICULTURE
SURPLUS MARKETING ADMINISTRATION
WASHINGTON, D. C.

FOOD STAMP PLAN

SURPLUS COMMODITIES BULLETIN

Announcer: Well, say, Mr. _____, I know of many people who would like to can, but can't, because they don't have the space at home, or the equipment, or both.

O.S.   The Community Canning Center in their neighborhood is the answer to their dilmma. For the last few years people who couldn't can at home have been going to their Community Canneries and have come home with wonderful results.

Announcer: The centers certainly do come in handy. I know our listeners who have never been to a canning center would like to know something about what they have to offer.

O.S.   Well, in the first place , the Community Canning Center is an excellent place for the novice canners to get their start. There they will begin to work under the guidance of a trained supervisor.

Announcer: And I bet that working with someone who knows the rope saves an awful lot of good food that would otherwise go to waste.

O. S.   One of the most important aspects of canning is to know the right methods to use for the specific foods that are to be put up. The supervisor at the canning center is there for just that purpose-guiding canners along the right path.

UNITED STATES DEPARTMENT OF AGRICULTURE
SURPLUS MARKETING ADMINISTRATION
WASHINGTON, D. C.

FOOD STAMP PLAN

SURPLUS COMMODITIES BULLETIN

Announcer: Knowing what to do, without fussing around and ex-
                perimenting also saves a lot of time, I should imagine.

O. S.   That is another advantage of the Community Canning Center.
                The center has its equipment set up in such a way that
                everything is done with the least possible loss of time.
                And speaking of equipment, that is another advantage that
                the centers offer canner. Many lack the right kind of
                equipment for successful preserving. By using the
                facilities of the canneries, they have everything they
                need right at their finger tips.

Announcer: And by going to a cannery, canners save the expense of
                buying equipment. But, Mr._____, is their any charge
                for the use of the cannery facilities?

O. S.   Many Community Canning Centers charge a small fee for the
                use of the equipment. And if foods are put up in tin cans,
                the cannery usually sell the cans for a slight charge.

Announcer: Well, if glass jars are used, does the center also supply
                them ?

O. S.
                No, in most cases, canners have to bring their own glass
                jars.

Announcer: And of course, they have to bring their own produce.

UNITED STATES DEPARTMENT OF AGRICULTURE
SURPLUS MARKETING ADMINISTRATION
WASHINGTON, D. C.

FOOD STAMP PLAN

SURPLUS COMMODITIES BULLETIN

O. S.   Usually. And right there is another advantage to using
        the centers. Quite often husbands and children go to the
        center to help carry the produce. And once they get
        there, they become interested in what's going on, and
        stay to help. But, if they were asked to help at home,
        they might put "thumbs down" on the idea.

Announcer:
        I suppose from a social standpoint, the canneries have
        something to offer, also.

O. S.   Indeed. they do. In the first place, it's always more fun
        to do things with other people. Then too, you can cement
        old friendships as well as make new ones. But that is
        just a small part of the advantage to be gained by going
        to the Community Canning Centers. Many of them not only
        have pressure cookers, but some of the larger ones have
        dehydrators and freezers, as well as tanks, retorts and
        sealers. Of course to get any real value from a freezer,
        you must have a cold storage locker in which to store
        your frozen foods.

Announcer: Well, say, Mr._____we've been discussing the Community
        Canning Centers as though every community had one. But,
        suppose there is someone listening in who would like to
        start one in his neighborhood. How would you suggest
        getting started?

UNITED STATES DEPARTMENT OF AGRICULTURE
SURPLUS MARKETING ADMINISTRATION
WASHINGTON, D. C.

FOOD STAMP PLAN
SURPLUS COMMODITIES BULLETIN

O. S. The first thing is to get together a group of interested people. Find out how many people will be using the center, how much food they plan on putting up and what kinds of foods they are interested in canning. Then you have to set up a planning committee. It's a good idea to have one good business person on the committee, for it's serious business. The committee should also include a health official, home economists, and people who are willing to work.

Announcer: Once you have a working committee, how do you go about financing the cannery?

O. S. That's one of the hardest jobs--getting funds. A good sponsor, like the Rotary or Kiwanis Clubs, help a great deal. If there is no non-profit civic organization in your town, funds may be raised from a loan from local citizens. The loan may be repaid by charging a small fee for the use of the center. The next important step is to select a suitable site for the center. Church basements are often turned into small canneries. School practice kitchens make good answers, too. Then, of course, study of buildings that are no longer used are also usually good sites. Old stores, garages and laundries often make fine centers, provided they have gas, electricity and running water.

UNITED STATES DEPARTMENT OF AGRICULTURE
SURPLUS MARKETING ADMINISTRATION
WASHINGTON, D. C.

FOOD STAMP PLAN
SURPLUS COMMODITIES BULLETIN

Announcer: Now that we are all set with our site, how would we go
               about getting a supervisor to guide us on to bigger and
               better canning?

O. S.   Well, the local home economics teachers would be as good
               a person as any. Your local county agricultural agent or
               State Agricultural College would probably be able to
               suggest a supervisor. Someone from a commercial cannery
               would be a big help. The important thing is to be sure
               that the supervisor is familar with commercial canning,
               as community canning is quite different from home
               canning.

Announcer:

               And now what about equipment, Mr. _____?

O. S.   Well, that all depends on the size of the center. If it's
               only going to be a small one a few pressure canners
               will probably be sufficient, but if it's 'a larger cannery,
               you will need more elaborate equipment in larger units.
               The USDA's Office of Supply has put out a fine bulletin
               covering every aspect of Community Canning Centers.

Announcer: How may this bulletin be obtained, Mr. _____?

O. S.   * Just write to the Office of Supply, CCC, United States
               Department of Agriculture, 150 Broadway, New York 7, New
               York.

UNITED STATES DEPARTMENT OF AGRICULTURE
SURPLUS MARKETING ADMINISTRATION
WASHINGTON, D. C.

FOOD STAMP PLAN

SURPLUS COMMODITIES BULLETIN

Announcer: Well, Mr. _____I'm sure that many of our listeners will want to take advantage of this offer. And people living in communities that already have Community Canning Centers will surely want to take advantage of them.

O. S.   Yes, the centers have much to offer. Canners may work under trained supervision, use equipment supplied by the canneries, save time and expense, and get to know their neighbors better. But wherever you live, if there is a community canning center near you, you should take advantage of it, provided that you don't can at home.

Announcer:
Thank you for being with us this morning, Mr. _____ of the USDA's Office of Supply. And folks, don't forget the bulletin entitled "Community Canning Centers". It's yours for the asking. Just write Office of Supply, CCC, U. S. Department of Agriculture, 150 Broadway, N. Y. 7, N. Y,, and mention the name of the station to which you are listening.

* To District and Sub-District Representatives: If you prefer to have request forwarded directly to your own office, we will supply you with extra bulletins- if you need them, Just substitute your local office for USDA's office in script.

UNITED STATES DEPARTMENT OF AGRICULTURE
SURPLUS MARKETING ADMINISTRATION
WASHINGTON, D. C.

FOOD STAMP PLAN

SURPLUS COMMODITIES BULLETIN

U. S. DEPARTMENT OF AGRICULTURE
OFFICE OF SUPPLY; CCC
150 Broadway, New York 7, N. Y.

Issued:
August 17, 1945

THE FAMILY CANTEEN

The Immediate Post-War Effect on Food

ANNOUNCER: The War is over. The world is at peace once more. However, now
that peace reigns again new problems come to mind. One of the
most often-thought-of questions is, now that the war is over,
how will the food situation be affected? To help us get a
glimpse into the food picture that is before use, we have with
us _____of the USDA's Office of
Supply. Mr._____, just what does peace mean to
our American diet? Will there be a radical change for the
better immediately, or will food, like many other commodities,
take a while to get back on it's peacetime feet?

OS: Well,_____, food comes in the last group--it will
be some time before food is available in the quantities it was
in pre-war years. Of course, food production has gone up
tremendously during the war, but then, too, so has demand. An
easing of the food situation in the United States will be a
combination of decreased civilian/demand and decreased government set-
asides for our Armed Forces on some foods, such as meat, eggs,
poultry, canned fruits and vegetables and evaporated milk. We
shall also see an improvement in civilian food supplies when
areas in other parts of the world are again producing such
commodities as fats and oils and sugar.

UNITED STATES DEPARTMENT OF AGRICULTURE
SURPLUS MARKETING ADMINISTRATION
WASHINGTON, D. C.

FOOD STAMP PLAN

SURPLUS COMMODITIES BULLETIN

ANNOUNCER: In other words it's a job of reconversion?

OS: That's **one** way of putting it.

ANNOUNCER: Well, getting back to the immediate food situation that faces us. Will the Armed Forces food requirements be drastically reduced now that the war is over?

OS: Not exactly. In the first place, the Army will still need food for the trainees here in this country. Then too, our occupation forces in Germany and Japan will require more food than they did as battle-field soldiers. No more K or C rations for these men. Occupation troops have more leisure for eating. They have the facilities for preparing food just as the Army cooks do here in camps in the United States.

ANNOUNCER: Well, I guess no soldier will be sorry to say good-bye to battle rations.

OS: Indeed, not. American soldiers all over the world will continue to receive the very best American food available. But they are not the **only** people scattered over the globe who depend on **us** for food.

ANNOUNCER: Are you referring to the recently liberated countries Mr._____?

OS: Yes, that's right. Countries, which less than a year ago were in the hands of the enemy, look to us for aid from starvation this coming winter. We cannot turn **our** back on our neighbors. A world at peace calls for contentment and to keep people happy they must be fed.

UNITED STATES DEPARTMENT OF AGRICULTURE
SURPLUS MARKETING ADMINISTRATION
WASHINGTON, D. C.

FOOD STAMP PLAN

SURPLUS COMMODITIES BULLETIN

ANNOUNCER: Speaking of sending food overseas, Mr._____what will
be the main product which will be exported this year?

OS: We have a bumper crop of wheat this year, so we shall be able
to share a large part of it with the hungry peoples of the
world.

ANNOUNCER: Well, getting down to specifice commodities, Mr._____. Just
how will the end of the war affect our sugar supplies?

OS: Sugar is one of the commodities that is going to remain short.
In the first place, our sugar resources in the Philippines have
to built up. That will take time. Also, this year's Cuban
sugar crop was cut by a drought. And then, too, the Eurpoean
countries have not been able to resume their pre-war production
of beet sugar. That means a continued scarcity of sugar for
the time being anyway.

ANNOUNCER: And what about fats and oils?

OS: Here we have one of the most critical problems which is
confronting the Nation. The fact that the war is over is not
going to help this situation for sometime to come.

ANNOUNCER: Why is that, Mr._____?

UNITED STATES DEPARTMENT OF AGRICULTURE
SURPLUS MARKETING ADMINISTRATION
WASHINGTON, D. C.

FOOD STAMP PLAN
SURPLUS COMMODITIES BULLETIN

OS: Well, in the first place, before the war America was an importer of fats and oils. When war came she turned to exporting these products. The South Pacific islands from which we get much of our oils are not expected to be producing copra, or coconut oil for at least 18 months. The same is true of the Philippine Islands. The Philippine processing mills were destroyed by the Japanese and the buildings will have to be repaired or rebuilt. The same holds true for the machinery. Also boats are needed to transport the copra, grown on the isolated islands, to the main islands for processing.

ANNOUNCER: Won't there be an easing of the fat supply by increased production of lard?

OS: Yes, but there won't be more lard until next spring or summer when the 1945 hog crop goes to market.

ANNOUNCER: Well, that sounds like an urgent need for more fat salvage.

OS: Yes, now more than ever before, Uncle Sam needs every pound of fat that the American housewife can save. Fats and oils go into the production of 111 essential products and of that number, the greatest majority is made up of civilian goods, things that people have been waiting for.

ANNOUNCER: That's just a case of our helping ourselves.

OS: Right.

ANNOUNCER: Will the meat situation be affected by the end of the war, Mr._____?

UNITED STATES DEPARTMENT OF AGRICULTURE
SURPLUS MARKETING ADMINISTRATION
WASHINGTON, D. C.

FOOD STAMP PLAN

SURPLUS COMMODITIES BULLETIN

OS: There probably will not be a great deal more meat for the civilian for quite a while. The meat stocks are low. Our Armed Forces will still come first. That's only right. They will need meat for our men stationed in Japan and Germany. However, Secretary of Agriculture Anderson recently signed an order which permits non-federally inspected slaughterers to sell their meats across state lines provided they comply with the sanitation rules set up, the price ceilings in force and provided they sell to legitimate markets. This step should mean more meat for civilians. But don't expect too many pre-war steaks for a while.

ANNOUNCER: And how about the poultry situation?

OS: We should be seeing some improvement. Effective August 13, dressed poultry in twelve midwest states is to be shared by the Army and civilians. The Quartermaster Corps has first choice of the top 50 per cent of all dressed poultry produced in this area. The remaining 50 per cent goes to civilians. The purpose of the order is to provide chicken for the Armed Forces and to protect the civilian supply.

ANNOUNCER: And how will the chicken be used which the Army takes?

OS: Most of it will be canned for military use.

ANNOUNCER: Speaking of chickens, how is our egg supply going to be now that the war is over?

(more)

UNITED STATES DEPARTMENT OF AGRICULTURE
SURPLUS MARKETING ADMINISTRATION
WASHINGTON, D. C.

FOOD STAMP PLAN

SURPLUS COMMODITIES BULLETIN

ANNOUNCER: Well, say, Mr._____,will there be more commercially canned
               fruits and vegetables for civilians?

OS: Supplies are improving. On August 5 the USDA announced a reduc-
               tion in set-asides of some canned fruits and canned vegetables.
               All in all, there will be approximately 10 per cent more, or __
                                     canned
               10 million more cases of/vegetables for civilians. However, to
               insure adequate supplies for next winter, the Department of
               Agriculture urges housewives to go full steam ahead with their
               canning.

ANNLUNCER: Speaking of canned products, will civilians now be able to get
               more evaporated milk?

OS: No. Canned milk will still be an essential military product.
               But civilians may look forward to continued good supplies of
               fresh milk.

ANNOUNCER: Well, that's good news. From what you have told us, it is
               plain to see the food situation is _not_ going to change rapidly.

OS: No. It will take some time to return to what it was in pre-war
               years. Our Armed Forces will still get first call on our food
               supplies. We shall have to sent some food to ward off starva-
               tion in the liberated countries. Sugar, fats and oils and eggs
               will remain tight. Meat and poultry should show some improvement.
               Our Armed Forces will continue to have first call on all com-
               mercially canned fruits and vegetables, so the wise housewife
               will continue to can all she can.

ANNOUNCER: Thank you for being with us this morning, Mr._____ of
               the USDA's Office of Supply.

                                    #

UNITED STATES DEPARTMENT OF AGRICULTURE
SURPLUS MARKETING ADMINISTRATION
WASHINGTON, D. C.

FOOD STAMP PLAN
SURPLUS COMMODITIES BULLETIN

THE FAMILY CANTEEN

A Vote of Thanks

ANNOUNCER: Food was a weapon of war. That may seem like a strange statement
to make when you consider war in terms of tanks, bombs and planes.
But the old adage that "an army moves on its stomach" is still
true, no matter how mechanized warfare may become. America went
all-out for war after Pearl Harbor. Her industries made rapid
changes from peacetime manufacture to wartime production. One
of America's chief industries, food, also went all out for war.
The farmers produced beyond their peactime capacity, food
processors and packers devoted much of their effort to food for
our armed forces and allies, the transportation companies put
their shoulders to the wheel to keep food moving to where it was
needed most, and housewives took out after out in rations and
watched their favorite commodities disappear from grocers'
shelves with the resolve to make the next best thing do. Today
we have with us _____ _____ of USDA's Office
of Supply. Mr. _____, don't you think that everyone
involved either in producing or serving food deserves a vote
of thanks?

OS: I do, indeed. Without the combined efforts of everybody, we
could never have reached the goal of food production that we
set for ourselves. Of course, the fellow who deserves most
credit is the farmer, for without his initial production of

vast quantities of food, the producer, packer and transporter would have had nothing to work on.

ANNOUNCER: And the housewife, in many instances, would not have had the food to serve in her daily menus or can for future use.

OS: But we must not forget the Victory Gardeners. They produced much of America's food.

ANNOUNCER: Well, let's take each in his turn and see how each contributed to Victory.

OS: As I said before, first, we have the farmer. He worked against odds probably experienced by no other group. His young farm hands and sons went off to war. He was left short handed.

ANNOUNCER: But the farm volunteers, such as the Women's Land Army and the Victory/Volunteers lent a helping hand to the hard-pressed farmer.

OS: Yes, without their help the farmer would have been greatly handicapped. But these groups contributed their services, as did so many volunteer war workers. Even so, it was not an easy job to go all out for production, especially with old farm machinery which couldn't be replaced, simple because there wasn't any new machinery being made.

ANNOUNCER: But the job was done. Once the food was harvested it found its way to market either for direct purchase for our dinner tables, or it was shipped to the food processing companies where it was canned, frozen, dehydrated or stored.

OS: The food processing plants did a mammoth job turning out high quality processed foods for our armed forces, our allies,

OS:
(CONT.)
and we civilians here on the home front. The USDA has recognized the fine work of such plants and their employees. Again we say thanks for the good work, and hope that they'll keep it up now that peace has come.

ANNOUNCER:
But without the efforts of the packers processed foods would not have been properly protected.

OS:
Hand in hand with the packers go the transportation industries and the distributive trades which actually placed food in the hands of our Armed Forces, and on our tables...packages were needed to hold and protect...while ships, trains and trucks delivered the goods.

ANNOUNCER:
And once it was delivered to local markets, homemakers went into action.

OS:
The housewife had a great responsibility on her hands. She had to plan her menus to fit what was available at the market and what she could buy with her ration stamps. She spent many long hours canning the produce which Dad had worked so hard over in his Victory garden. Or else she took advantage of abundant foods while they were in season.

ANNOUNCER:
But there were other sides to food on the wartime home front.

OS:
Yes, we must not forget the many substitutes which Mrs. America served for our favorite dishes. You know, I'll bet lots of folks have gotten to like things which before the war they'd never have dreamed of eating.

ANNOUNCER:
And we mustn't forget our war against waste.

OS: Many of us signed up for "The Clean Platter Club", and vowed to combat food waste. Speaking of conservation brings us to the housewife's valiant efforts to salvage all the used fats she could.

ANNOUNCER: But that's a job that must still go on—even though the war is over.

OS: Yes, indeed. We are now facing our most critical fats and oils shortage. Every drop of used kitchen fat must be salvaged... no matter how old or dirty it may seem. If you have any used kitchen fat which you can't use for cooking purposes, put it in a tin can and when you have a pound, take it to your butcher or grocer.

ANNOUNCER: And those two red ration points will still seem good.

OS: Getting back to the war for a moment. Food, you know, was not only a weapon of war to keep our armies well fed and in good spirits, but it was a morale builder for our allies and the civilians of the liberated countries.

ANNOUNCER: Yes, we all remember pictures of American G I's handing out food to half-starved civilians soon after they'd captured a town.

OS: And none of us will forget the newsreel shots of the happy expressions on kids faces as American soldiers give them their precious chocolate rations. Yes, some of the chocolate that we looked for in vain at our local candy dealers went a long way in erasing the horror of years of hunger and opression.

ANNOUNCER: And that brings us down to present day needs for food by
            our allies in the recently liberated countries.

OS: If you are referring to the need for American aid to help
            the liberated peoples of the world from starving this coming
            winter, you're right. We cannot let up now. In the first
            place our armed forces still have first call on most foods.
            And, as citizens of the world we must do our part to help
            feed those not as well off as we.

ANNOUNCER: Didn't President Truman say something about our aid to
            foreign nations?

OS: Yes, just about seven weeks ago the President said, "Beyond
            our tremendous military requirements lies the task of
            working with other nations to help liberated peoples regain
            strength and rebuild their countries. There can be no
            lasting peace in a hungry world."

ANNOUNCER: Yes sir, food is a tool of peace we can't afford to ignore.

OS: And speaking of peace, we should be seeing some new develop-
            ments in foods which are the result of wartime research.
            Great strides have been made in food preservation. Quick
            freezing of fruits, vegetables and meats. Dehydration of
            fruits and vegetables will add new, convenient items to
            the family larder, and air transportation will make fresh
            food available from distant points. But it's going to be
            a slow process, and we must all be patient. America has
            won a great battle not only on the field but also here at

OS:
(Cont.)   home. Wartime production, and especially food production and

preservation are something of which we can all be proud.

ANNOUNCER: We can, indeed, Mr._____. Thank you for being with

us today. You have just been listening to_____ _____

of the USDA's Office of Supply.

CPSIA information can be obtained
at www.ICGtesting.com
Printed in the USA
BVHW040259121218
535228BV00033BA/1977/P